Using the Standards
Geometry

Grade 5

Published by Instructional Fair
an imprint of
Frank Schaffer Publications®

Instructional Fair

Development House: MATHQueue, Inc.

Frank Schaffer Publications®

Instructional Fair is an imprint of Frank Schaffer Publications.

Send all inquiries to:
Frank Schaffer Publications
8720 Orion Place
Columbus, OH 43240-2111

Using the Standards: Geometry—Grade 5

ISBN: 0-7424-2985-7

3 4 5 6 7 8 9 10 POH 10 09 08 07

Table of Contents

0-7424-2985-7 *Using the Standards: Geometry*

Introduction

This book is designed around the standards from the National Council of Teachers of Mathematics (NCTM) with a focus on geometry. Students will build new mathematical knowledge, solve problems in context, apply and adapt appropriate strategies, and reflect on processes.

The NCTM process standards are also incorporated throughout the activities. The correlation chart on page 6 identifies the pages on which each NCTM geometry substandard appears. Also look for the following process icons on each page.

 Problem Solving   Communication   Reasoning and Proof

 Connections   Representation

Workbook Pages: These activities can be done independently, in pairs, or in groups. The problems are designed to stimulate higher-level thinking skills and address a variety of learning styles.

Problems may be broken into parts with class discussion following student work. At times solution methods or representations are suggested in the activities. Students may gravitate toward using these strategies, but they should also be encouraged to create and share their own strategies.

Many activities will lead into subjects that could be investigated or discussed further as a class. You may want to compare different solution methods or discuss how to select a valid solution method for a particular problem.

Communication: Most activities have a communication section. These questions may be used as journal prompts, writing activities, or discussion prompts. Each communication question is labeled **THINK** or **DO MORE**.

Create Your Own Problems: These pages prompt students to create problems like those they completed on the workbook pages. Encourage students to be creative and to use their everyday experiences. The students' responses will help you to assess their practical knowledge of the topic.

                    0-7424-2985-7 *Using the Standards: Geometry*

Introduction (cont.)

Check Your Skills: These activities provide a representative sample of the types of problems developed throughout each section. These can be used as additional practice or as assessment tools.

Vocabulary Cards: Use the vocabulary cards to familiarize students with mathematical language. The pages may be copied, cut, and pasted onto index cards. Paste the front and back on the same index card to make flash cards, or paste each side on separate cards to use in matching games or activities.

Assessment: Assessment is an integral part of the learning process and can include observations, conversations, interviews, interactive journals, writing prompts, and independent quizzes or tests. Classroom discussions help students learn the difference between poor, good, and excellent responses. Scoring guides can help analyze students' responses. The following is a possible list of problem-solving steps. Modify this list as necessary to fit specific problems.

1—Student understands the problem and knows what he or she is being asked to find.

2—Student selects an appropriate strategy or process to solve the problem.

3—Student is able to model the problem with appropriate manipulatives, graphs, tables, pictures, or computations.

4—Student is able to clearly explain or demonstrate his or her thinking and reasoning.

Published by Instructional Fair. Copyright protected.   0-7424-2985-7 *Using the Standards: Geometry*

NCTM Standards Correlation Chart

		Problem Solving	Reasoning and Proof	Communication	Connections	Representation
Relationships	identify and analyze 2-D and 3-D shapes	13, 14, 22,	11, 12, 14, 19,	9, 10, 11, 13, 15,	12, 15, 21,	9, 10, 16, 17, 18,
	classify shapes	23, 33, 34,	21, 25, 26, 27,	16, 17, 18, 23, 25,	29, 30, 31	19, 20, 24, 26,
	subdivide and combine 2-D and 3-D shapes		28, 32, 33, 35	27, 30, 31, 32,		28, 29, 35, 36
	explore congruence and similarity	37, 38		36, 37, 38		
	make and test conjectures					
Locations	describe location and movement	43, 44, 54	51, 53, 54,	42, 43, 44, 55,	42, 45,	45, 46, 47, 48, 49, 50,
	use coordinate grids		59, 61	56, 58, 59, 61	46, 55	51, 52, 57, 58, 60
	find horizontal and vertical distance					
Transformations	predict and describe flips, slides, and turns	68, 71, 75	66, 68, 71,	65, 67, 72,	66, 73,	65, 67, 69,
	show congruence using motion		73, 74, 75,	76, 77	77, 78	70, 72, 74
	identify line and rotational symmetry		76, 78			
Modeling	build and draw geometric objects	96, 97, 98,	86, 91, 94	85, 86, 91,	82, 87, 98,	82, 83, 84, 85, 87,
	identify 2-D representations of 3-D objects	99, 100, 101,		95, 97, 100	101, 102, 105	88, 89, 90, 92,
	use models to solve problems in number and measurement	102, 104, 105				93, 95, 96,
	apply geometry in everyday life					99, 103, 104

The pretest, post test, Create Your Own Problems, and Check Your Skills pages are not included on this chart, but contain a representative sampling of the process standards. Many pages also contain THINK or DO MORE sections, which encourage students to communicate about what they have learned.

0-7424-2985-7 *Using the Standards: Geometry*

Pretest

1. Draw a line so that it is perpendicular to the line given.

2. Draw a regular hexagon.

3. Which solid figure is a cylinder?

Figure A   Figure B   _____

4. Name the ordered pair for each vertex of the triangle.

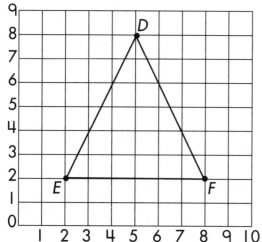

D _____

E _____

F _____

5. What type of triangle is shown on the coordinate grid? _____

0-7424-2985-7 *Using the Standards: Geometry*

Pretest (cont.)

6. How many lines of symmetry does this plane figure have? Draw these lines.

_____

7. What is the length (in units) of the base of triangle *LMN*?

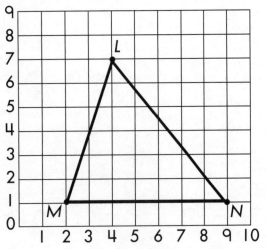

_____

8. Which transformation was performed on the letter P?

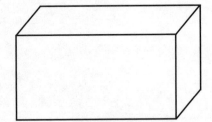

_____

9. How many faces, edges, and vertices does a rectangular prism have?

faces _____

edges _____

vertices _____

0-7424-2985-7 *Using the Standards: Geometry*

Name_____ Date _____

Segments, Rays, and Lines

A **line** goes on forever in both directions.

A **segment** is a part of a line. It has two endpoints.

A **ray** is a part of a line with one endpoint.
It goes on forever in only one direction.

Directions: Use a ruler to draw each figure in the space provided.

1. a line segment that is 2 inches long

2. a ray

3. a line

4. a line segmer   centimeters long

THINK

Can you draw a line 4 inches long? Explain why or why not.

Name_____ Date _____

Classify Lines

Parallel lines never intersect.

Intersecting lines cross at one point.

Perpendicular lines intersect to form right angles. (90 degrees)

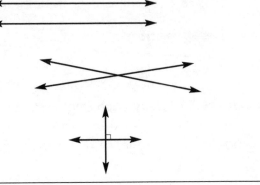

Directions: Sketch the indicated line through the point given.

1.   an intersecting line

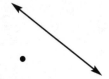

2.   a parallel line

3.   a perpendicular line

4.   a perpendicular line

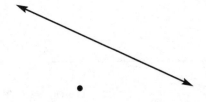

THINK

Suppose line *a* is perpendicular to line *b*, and line b is perpendicular to line *c*. What is the relationship between lines *a* and *c*? Sketch lines *a*, *b*, and *c* to support your answer.

Name_____ Date_____

Classify and Measure Angles

An angle that forms a square corner (90°) is a **right angle.**

An angle that has a measure less than 90° is an **acute angle**.

An angle that has a measure greater than 90° is an **obtuse angle**.

Directions: Classify each angle. Then use a protractor to find the measure of each angle.

1.

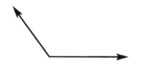

_____ _____ °

2.

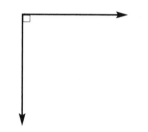

_____ _____ °

3.

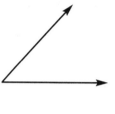

_____ _____ °

4.

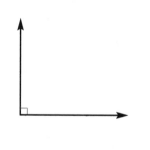

_____ _____ °

5.

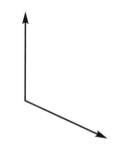

_____ _____ °

6.

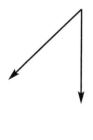

_____ _____ °

THINK

When two rays extend in opposite directions, they form a straight angle. What is the measure of a straight angle?

Name_____ Date _____

Modeling with Lines

Directions: Use the map below to answer the following questions.

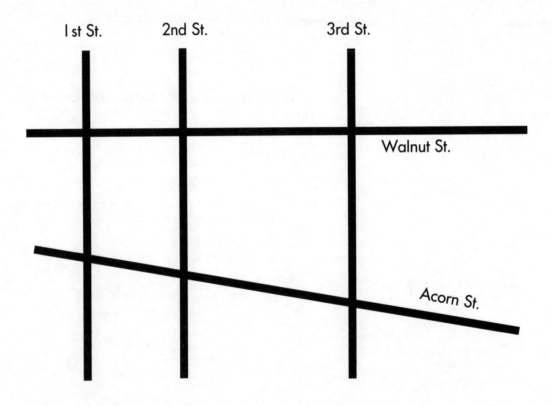

1. What type of lines do 1st Street and Walnut Street appear to form?

   _____

2. What type of lines do 2nd Street and 3rd Street appear to form?

   _____

3. What type of lines do 3rd Street and Acorn Street form?

   _____

4. If Walnut Street and Acorn Street are extended, what type of lines will they form?

   _____

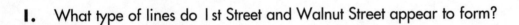

Name_____ Date _____

Finding Angles in Numbers

Directions: Some numbers are made with line segments that form angles.
Three examples are shown below.

7	4	1
right 0	right 4	right 0
acute 1	acute 2	acute 1
obtuse 0	obtuse 0	obtuse 0

Use the numbers shown below to answer the following questions.

0 1 2 3 4 5 6 7 8 9

1. How many right, acute, and obtuse angles are in your zip code?

right _____

acute _____

obtuse _____

2. How many right, acute, and obtuse angles are in your phone number?

right _____

acute _____

obtuse _____

0-7424-2985-7 *Using the Standards: Geometry*

Name_____ Date _____

Seeing Geometry in Words

Directions: The line segments used to form the letters of the alphabet sometimes form right angles, acute angles, and obtuse angles. They can also model parallel lines and perpendicular lines. For example, the letter E forms 4 right angles, 3 pairs of perpendicular lines, and 3 pairs of parallel lines.

A B C D E F G
H I J K L M N
O P Q R S T U
V W X Y Z

1. How many acute angles are in the name NANCY? _____

2. How many obtuse angles are in the name KATHY? _____

3. Which name has more right angles, TATE or LENNY? _____

4. How many pairs of perpendicular lines are in the word MATH? _____

5. How many pairs of parallel lines are in the word FERN? _____

DO MORE

Count the number of acute, right, and obtuse angles in your first name.

0-7424-2985-7 *Using the Standards: Geometry*

Name_____ Date _____

Angles on a Clock Face

Directions: The hands on a clock form different angles at different times. Draw minute and hour hands on the clock faces to solve each problem.

1. Show three different times where the minute and hour hands form an acute angle.

2. Show three different times where the minute and hour hands form an obtuse angle.

3. Show three different times where the minute and hour hands form a right angle.

THINK

Name the time where the minute and hour hands model a straight angle.

0-7424-2985-7 *Using the Standards: Geometry*

Name_____ Date _____

Identify Polygons

A **polygon** is a closed plane figure that is formed by three or more line segments.

Directions: Decide whether or not each figure is a polygon. Write yes or no.
If a figure is not a polygon, explain why not.

1.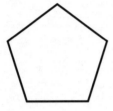

_____

2.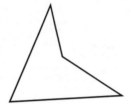

_____

3.

_____

4.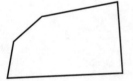

_____

5.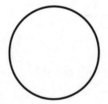

_____

6.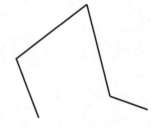

_____

THINK

 Name three objects in your classroom that model polygons.

etry

Name_____ Date _____

Draw Quadrilaterals

Directions: Draw a polygon to match each description.

1. A **quadrilateral** is a polygon with 4 sides.

2. A **parallelogram** is a quadrilateral with both pairs of opposite sides parallel to each other.

3. A **rectangle** is a parallelogram with 4 right angles.

4. A **square** is a parallelogram with 4 right angles and 4 equal sides.

5. A **rhombus** is a parallelogram with 4 equal sides.

6. A **trapezoid** is a quadrilateral with exactly one pair of parallel sides.

THINK

 True or False: A square is also a rectangle. Explain.

0-7424-2985-7 *Using the Standards: Geometry*

Plane Figures

Plane figures are figures that have two dimensions.
They can be classified by their number of sides.
Some common plane figures are triangles, quadrilaterals,
pentagons, hexagons, and octagons.

Directions: Tell how many sides each plane figure has.
Draw an example of each plane figure.

1. triangle _____ sides

2. quadrilateral _____ sides

3. pentagon _____ sides

4. hexagon _____ sides

5. octagon _____ sides

0-7424-2985-7 *Using the Standards: Geometry*

Name_____ Date _____

Regular Polygons

> **Regular polygons** are polygons with sides of equal length and angles of equal measure. Polygons that are not regular are irregular figures.

Directions: Determine if each polygon is a regular figure. Write regular or irregular. If a figure is irregular, explain why.

I.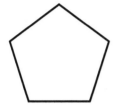

2.

3.

_____   _____   _____

4.

5.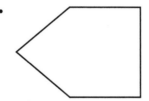

6.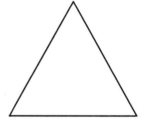

_____   _____   _____

THINK

Is it possible to draw a square that is not a regular figure? Explain why or why not.

0-7424-2985-7 *Using the Standards: Geometry*

Sides and Vertices

Each **side** of a polygon is a line segment.
The point where two sides of a polygon meet is a **vertex**.

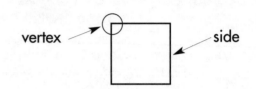

Vertices is the plural form of vertex.

Directions: How many vertices does each figure have?
How many sides does each figure have?

1.

_____ vertices

_____ sides

2.

_____ vertices

_____ sides

3.

_____ vertices

_____ sides

4.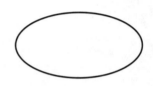

_____ vertices

_____ sides

5.

_____ vertices

_____ sides

6.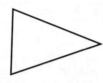

_____ vertices

_____ sides

THINK

 A septagon is a 7-sided polygon. How many vertices does a septagon have? Explain how you know.

0-7424-2985-7 *Using the Standards: Geometry*

Name_____ Date _____

Plane Figures in Drawings

Directions: List plane figure(s) that were used to create each drawing.

1.

_____

_____

2.

_____

_____

3.

_____

_____

4.

_____

_____

0-7424-2985-7 *Using the Standards: Geometry*

Name_____ Date _____

Polygon Puzzle

Directions: Cut out each of the shapes at the bottom of the page.
Arrange them to form a rectangle to match the rectangle at the top of the page.

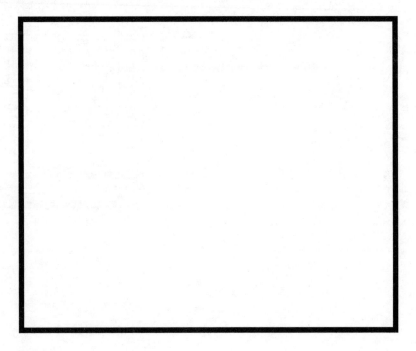

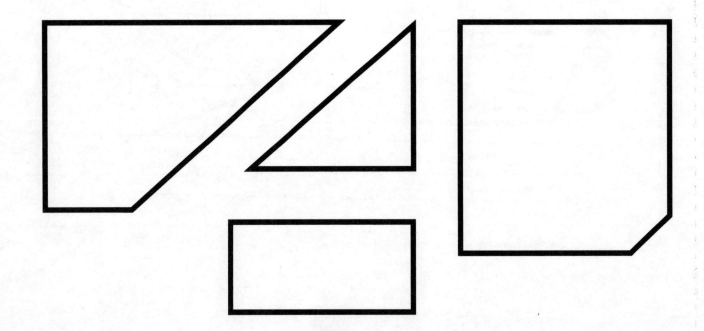

0-7424-2985-7 *Using the Standards: Geometry*

Name_____ Date _____

Polygon Puzzle, Part II

Directions: Cut out each of the shapes at the bottom of the page. Arrange them to form a trapezoid to match the trapezoid at the top of the page.

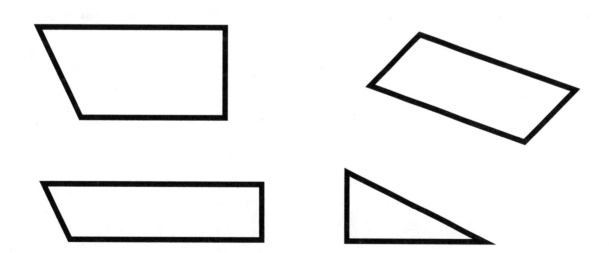

0-7424-2985-7 *Using the Standards: Geometry*

Name_____ Date_____

Types of Triangles

An **equilateral triangle** has 3 equal sides.

An **isosceles triangle** has 2 equal sides.

A **scalene triangle** has no equal sides.

Directions: Use a ruler to draw each figure.

1. an isosceles triangle with two 2-inch sides

2. a scalene triangle with a 3-inch side

3. a scalene triangle with a 5-centimeter side

4. an equilateral triangle with 2.5-inch sides

THINK

Is an equilateral triangle also an isosceles triangle?
Explain why or why not.

0-7424-2985-7 *Using the Standards: Geometry*

Name_____ Date_____

Definitions of Plane Figures

Directions: Complete the definition for each plane figure.

1. A square is a quadrilateral with 2 pairs of

_____ sides, 4 right angles, and 4 equal sides.

2. A _____ triangle has 3 sides of different lengths.

3. A rectangle is a quadrilateral with 2 pairs of parallel sides

and 4 _____ angles.

4. An _____ triangle has 3 equal sides.

5. A _____ is a quadrilateral with 2 pairs of parallel sides.

6. A trapezoid is a quadrilateral with 1 pair of _____ sides.

0-7424-2985-7 *Using the Standards: Geometry*

Name_____ Date _____

Sketch Triangles and Quadrilaterals

Directions: Use each description to sketch a plane figure. Write the name of each figure.

1. My 3 sides all have the same length. What am I?

_____

2. I have two pairs of parallel sides, but no right angles. What am I?

_____

3. Two of my three sides have the same length. My third side is half this length. What am I?

_____

4. I have four sides of equal length, but no right angles. What am I?

_____

0-7424-2985-7 *Using the Standards: Geometry*

Name_____ Date _____

Properties of Quadrilaterals

Directions: Identify each quadrilateral described. Sketch the quadrilateral near each box in the diagram.

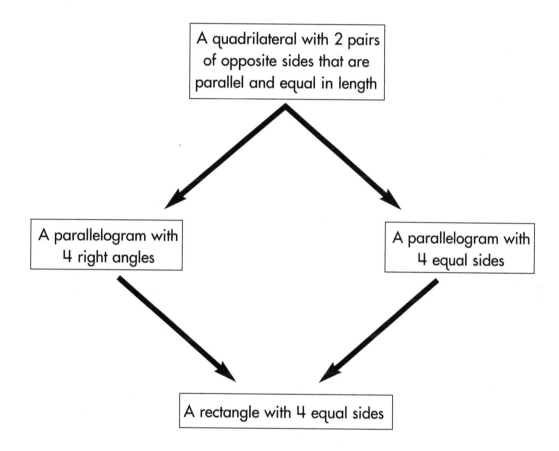

A quadrilateral with 2 pairs of opposite sides that are parallel and equal in length

A parallelogram with 4 right angles

A parallelogram with 4 equal sides

A rectangle with 4 equal sides

DO MORE

Use the diagram to answer the following True/False questions:

1. A square is also a rhombus.

2. A parallelogram is also a rectangle.

0-7424-2985-7 *Using the Standards: Geometry*

Name_____ Date _____

Faces and Edges of Solid Figures

A **face** is the flat surface of a solid figure.

The place where two faces of a solid figure meet is an **edge**.

The point where two edges meet is a **vertex**.

vertex

edge

face

Directions: Write the name of each solid figure in the first column.
Then complete the table.

Solid Figure	Number of Faces	Number of Edges	Number of Vertices	Shape(s) of Faces
1.				
2.				
3.				
4.				
5.				

0-7424-2985-7 *Using the Standards: Geometry*

Name_____ Date _____

Identify Solid Figures

Directions: Answer the following questions about Figures 1–5.

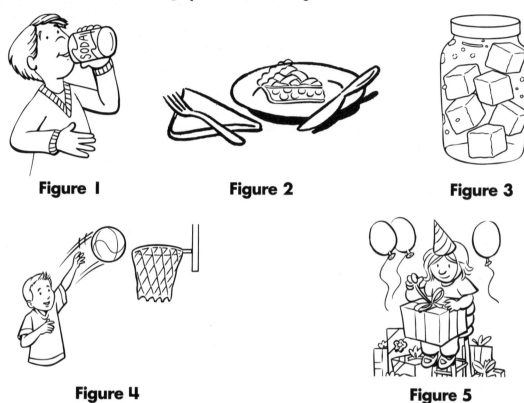

Figure 1   **Figure 2**   **Figure 3**

Figure 4   **Figure 5**

1. In which figures are there rectangular prisms or cubes?

_____

2. In which figures are there triangular prisms?

_____

3. In which figure is there a cylinder?

_____

4. In which figures are there spheres?

_____

29

Name_____ Date _____

Identify Solid Figures Around You

Directions: Name three objects that you see in your home or at school that model the following solid figures.

1. cube _____

_____

_____

2. cylinder _____

_____

_____

3. rectangular prism _____

_____

_____

4. cone _____

_____

_____

0-7424-2985-7 *Using the Standards: Geometry*

Name_____ Date _____

Identify Solid Figures Around You, Part II

Directions: Many objects around you are made up of more than one solid figure. For example, a jar that is shaped like a cylinder may be filled with ice cubes. Name three objects that you see in your home or at school that model more than one solid figure. Name the object, and tell what solid figures are modeled.

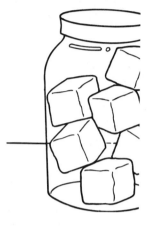

1. Object #1

_____

_____

2. Object #2

_____

_____

3. Object #3

_____

_____

0-7424-2985-7 *Using the Standards: Geometry*

Name_____ Date _____

Solid Figure Detective

Directions: Use the clues to name each solid figure described.
Sketch each solid figure.

1. I have 1 circular base and 1 vertex.

_____

2. I have 5 faces altogether, and 2 of them are triangles.

_____

3. I have 2 circular bases that are parallel to each other.

_____

4. I have 4 congruent faces.

_____

5. I have 6 faces that all have the same shape and size.

_____

DO MORE

Write a clue that describes a sphere. Have a friend read the clue and see if
he or she can guess the solid figure correctly.

0-7424-2985-7 *Using the Standards: Geometry*

Name_____ Date _____

Stacking Solid Figures

Directions: Benjamin is playing with his nephew's blocks. He wants to see which ones he is able to stack on top of each other. Tell whether or not the following sequence of blocks is able to be stacked on top of each other. Explain.

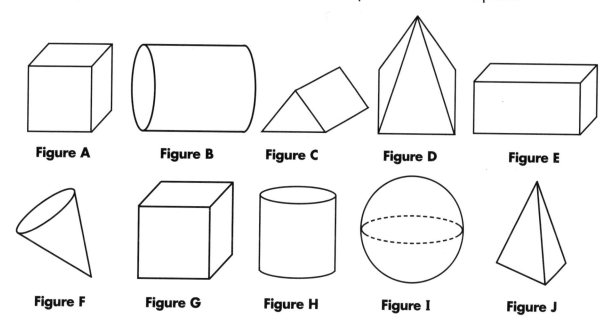

Figure A   **Figure B**   **Figure C**   **Figure D**   **Figure E**

Figure F   **Figure G**   **Figure H**   **Figure I**   **Figure J**

1. A - C - E - H - J _____

_____

2. B - F - J - C _____

_____

3. E - G - H - B - A - C - D _____

_____

THINK

Which block of a solid figure can never be stacked? Are there any solid figures that can only be stacked on top of other solid figures? Explain.

0-7424-2985-7 *Using the Standards: Geometry*

Name_____ Date _____

Follow the Path

Directions: The table shows several solid figures and plane figures. Trace a path from start to finish as described in questions 1 and 2. With each step, you may move one figure to the right, left, above, below, or at a diagonal.

1. Your path from start to finish may only pass over solid figures.

2. Your path from start to finish must alternate between solid figures and plane figures.

Start

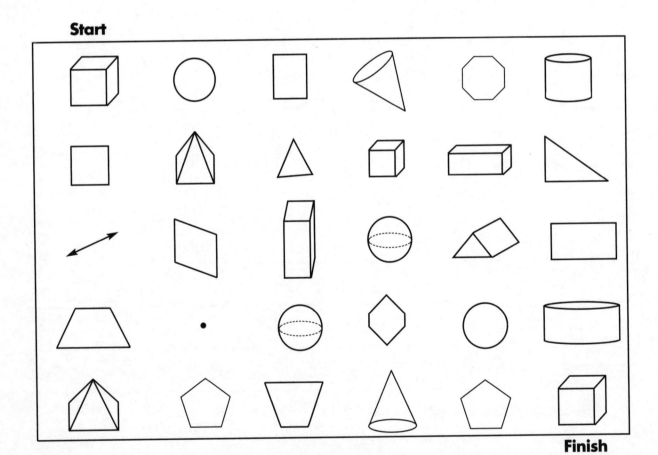

Finish

Published by Instructional Fair. Copyright protected.

0-7424-2985-7 *Using the Standards: Geometry*

Name_____ Date _____

Similar Figures

Similar figures have the same shape, and their sides are in proportion to each other.

Similar figures can be the same size.

Corresponding sides of similar polygons have lengths that are proportional.
Corresponding angles of similar polygons have equal measures.

Directions: Each pair of figures is similar. Find the unknown length.

1.

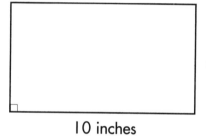

5 inches

10 inches

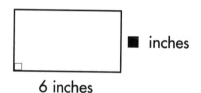

■ inches

6 inches

2.

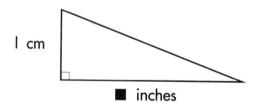

1 cm

■ inches

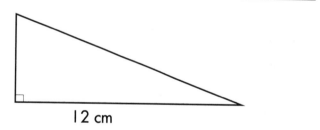

3 cm

12 cm

_____

3.

4 feet

4 feet

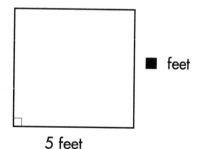

■ feet

5 feet

_____

_____

0-7424-2985-7 *Using the Standards: Geometry*

Name_____ Date _____

Draw Shapes with Symmetry

Directions: Draw the missing half of each figure so that the result is a symmetrical figure.

THINK

Name some letters of the alphabet that have symmetry.

How many letters in your name are symmetrical?

0-7424-2985-7 *Using the Standards: Geometry*

Name_____ Date _____

Word Scramble

Directions: Unscramble the following words. Then use this list of words in the Scramble Word Search on page 38.

1. LECRIC _____

2. DSOIL _____

3. LARPALOMRLGEA _____

4. OCEN _____

5. YMESMYRT _____

6. ANGTLIRE _____

7. OBURMSH _____

8. PIRMS _____

9. EANRTGLCE _____

10. QUASER _____

11. YPIDRMA _____

12. LPAEN _____

13. TERVEX _____

14. UBCE _____

15. AFEC _____

16. GEDE _____

0-7424-2985-7 *Using the Standards: Geometry*

Scramble Word Search

Directions: Find and circle each word from your list of unscrambled words on page 37.

```
P  R  I  S  M  D  P  Y  R  A  M  I  D  X
A  O  I  Q  F  Q  M  W  F  R  S  Y  L  A
R  G  H  U  E  T  F  J  L  E  S  A  Z  R
A  N  V  A  W  Q  A  H  B  C  O  N  E  H
L  O  P  R  T  Y  C  F  D  T  L  K  L  U
L  W  G  E  D  G  E  S  J  A  I  X  V  Y
E  K  R  L  T  E  W  Y  M  N  D  L  C  I
L  H  H  D  F  S  A  M  B  G  U  I  U  T
O  Y  O  G  P  N  A  M  P  L  N  R  B  W
G  F  M  C  L  K  X  E  V  E  R  T  E  X
R  C  B  S  A  G  K  T  L  W  F  C  S  J
A  M  U  R  N  G  T  R  I  A  N  G  L  E
M  V  S  A  E  F  T  Y  C  I  R  C  L  E
```

0-7424-2985-7 *Using the Standards: Geometry*

Name_____ Date _____

Create Your Own Problems

1. Write a word problem that involves two similar figures.

2. Write a question about the relationship between rectangles, squares, parallelograms, and rhombuses.

3. Write a question about an isosceles triangle. Include information about the lengths of the sides and the measures of the angles.

4. Write a question about items in your classroom that have symmetry.

5. Write a question about real world objects that model parallel lines, perpendicular lines, and intersecting lines.

0-7424-2985-7 *Using the Standards: Geometry*

Name_____ Date _____

Check Your Skills

1. Use a ruler to draw an isosceles triangle with two sides 3 centimeters long.

2. Draw a regular hexagon. What do you know about the sides and angles of this figure?

_____

_____

3. Name the solid figure with three rectangular faces and two triangular faces. Explain your reasoning.

_____

_____

4. Draw two similar right triangles in the space below. Label the lengths of the sides, and show that the figures are similar.

0-7424-2985-7 *Using the Standards: Geometry*

Name_____ Date _____

Check Your Skills (cont.)

5. How many faces does a triangular pyramid have? How many edges?
How many vertices?

_____   _____   _____

6. Which solid has six square faces?

_____

7. How many lines of symmetry does a regular octagon have?

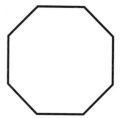

_____

8. Circle the solid figures that can be stacked in any position of a tower
of blocks that model solid figures.

| triangular prism | cylinder | cube | triangular pyramid |
| rectangular prism | sphere | cone | rectangular pyramid |

9. Which solid figure has only one circular face?

_____

10. Which numbers have no lines of symmetry?

0   I   2   3   4   5   6   7   8   9

_____

0-7424-2985-7 *Using the Standards: Geometry*

Name_____ Date _____

Around the Neighborhood

Directions: Use the grid below to answer the following questions. The grid lines represent streets, and each square represents one city block. To move from one location to another, move either horizontally or vertically along the grid lines.

park

library

store

school

beach

zoo

1. How many blocks is the school from the library? _____

2. After leaving the beach, Aaron went to the grocery store. Trace the shortest path between these locations. How many blocks did he travel? _____

3. Kim's class took a field trip to the zoo. How many blocks from the school is the zoo? _____

4. Which two locations in the town are the shortest distance apart? _____

THINK

Is there more than 1 way to travel from the park to the grocery store and travel the same number of blocks? Explain.

0-7424-2985-7 *Using the Standards: Geometry*

Name_____ Date _____

Secret Hideout

Directions: Andrea and her friends have a secret hideout for their club. It is located somewhere in her backyard.

Use the map on page 44 to answer the following questions and find the location of the club's secret hideout. Each block represents 1 meter.

1. Start at D1 and travel 2 meters east.
At what location on the map are you now?   _____

2. Go south to the dog house.
How many meters did you walk from the previous spot?   _____

3. Travel 2 meters east and 5 meters north.
What is your current location on the map?   _____

4. Go to the flower garden How far did you travel?   _____

5. Travel 3 meters north and 3 meters east. This is the location of the secret hideout. Name the location on the map of the secret hideout?   _____

0-7424-2985-7 *Using the Standards: Geometry*

Secret Hideout

Directions: Use the directions on page 43 to find the location of the secret hideout.

	1	2	3	4	5	6	7	8	9	10	11
A											
B					🟫						
C											🪑
D	X										
E											
F								🌸			
G			🏠								
H											

🏠 doghouse

🌸 flower garden

 sandbox

🪑 swing set

N
W — E
S

0-7424-2985-7 *Using the Standards: Geometry*

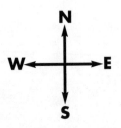

Name_____ Date _____

Nuts About Newspapers

Directions: This is a game for two players. You need 10 counters, 5 of one color, 5 of another. Each player selects 5 counters of the same color. These will represent newspapers. Use the game board on page 46.

Cut out the squares below and place them face down in a stack.

Players take turns drawing a single card from the stack.

If the card has an ordered pair, place one of your newspapers on the house located at the ordered pair. If your opponent has already placed a newspaper at that house, then your turn is over. If the card does not have an ordered pair, then follow the instructions on the card. At the end of each turn, return your card to the bottom of the stack.

Object of the game: Be the first player to deliver 5 newspapers to homes on the grid.

Game Cards

(6, 2)	(3, 4)	(8, 7)	(4, 1)
(2, 2)	(1, 7)	(7, 5)	(5, 6)
(8, 1)	(1, 4)	Take a rest.	Draw another card.
Put a paper at any house.	Skip a Turn.	Take a rest.	Draw another card.

0-7424-2985-7 *Using the Standards: Geometry*

Nuts About Newspapers

Directions: This is a game board for the game described on page 45.

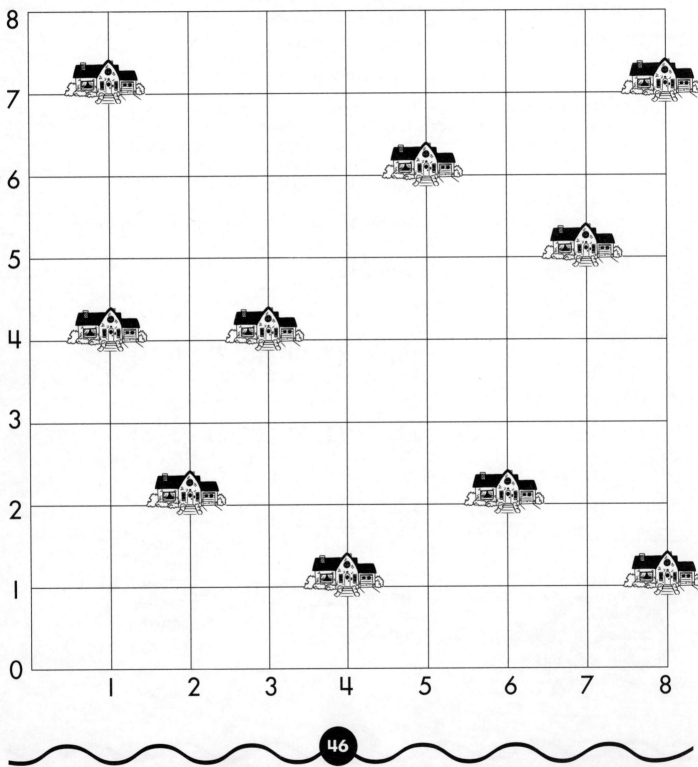

0-7424-2985-7 *Using the Standards: Geometry*

Name_____ Date _____

Drawing with Coordinates

Directions: Follow the instructions and answer the questions below.

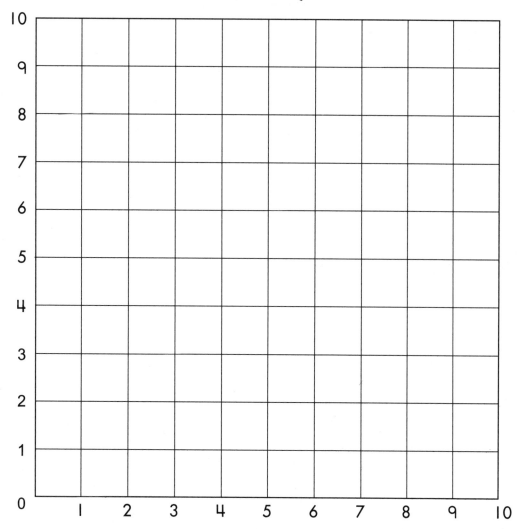

1. Plot the following ordered pairs: (2, 1) (2, 8) (4, 8) (5.5, 7) (7, 8) (9, 8) (9, 1)
(7, 1) (7, 5) (5.5, 3) (4, 5) (4, 1) (2, 1)

2. Connect the points in the order they are listed.

3. What letter did you draw?   _____

Name_____ Date _____

Draw a Solid Figure

Directions: Use the grid to plot the ordered pairs below. Then connect the points in the order in which they are listed.

(10, 9)	(5, 5)	(1, 5)	(6, 9)	(10, 9)	(10, 6)
(5, 2)	(1, 2)	(1, 5)	(5, 5)	(5, 2)	

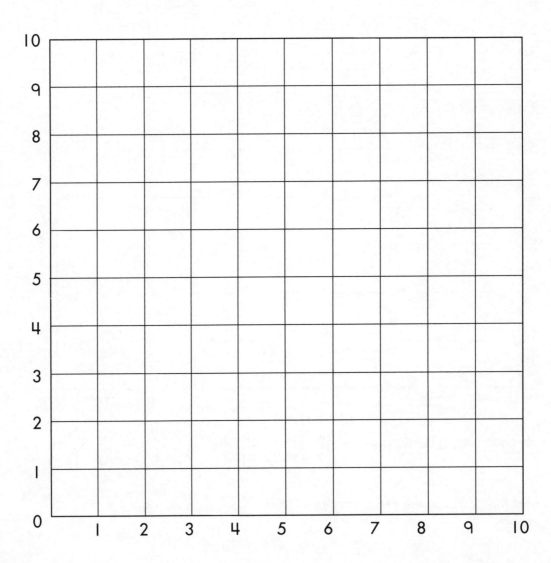

What type of solid figure did you draw? _____

Name_____ Date _____

Name the Vertices

Directions: Name the ordered pair for each vertex of the shapes shown.

1.

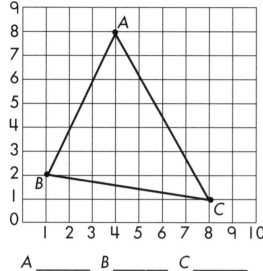

A_____ B_____ C_____

2.

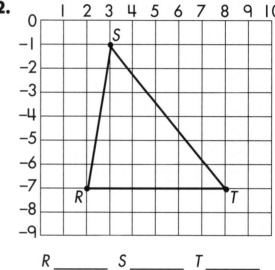

R_____ S_____ T_____

3.

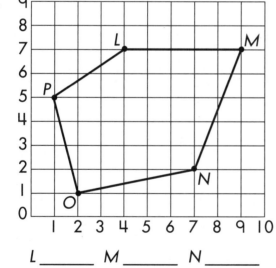

L_____ M_____ N_____

O_____ P_____

4.

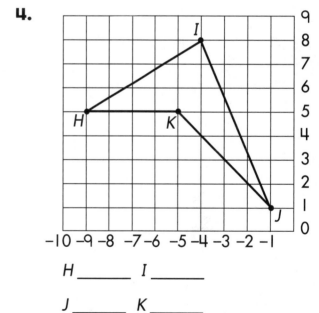

H_____ I_____

J_____ K_____

eometry

Name_____ Date _____

One Point Included

Directions: Graph each figure on a coordinate grid.

1. Graph an isosceles triangle that has one side 4 units long and one vertex at (2, 4).

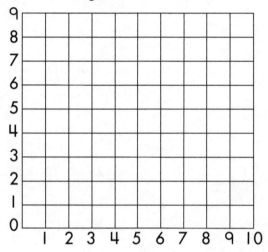

2. Graph a parallelogram with a base 5 units long and one vertex at (1, -2).

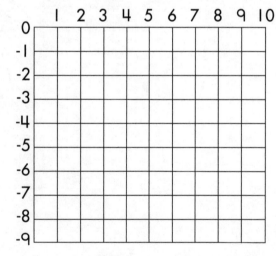

0-7424-2985-7 *Using the Standards: Geometry*

Name_____ Date _____

Graphing Ordered Pairs

Directions: Plot the ordered pairs on the coordinate grid. Then answer the following questions.

1. A(8, 3.5) **2.** B(1, 2)

3. C(2, 3) **4.** D(3, 4)

5. E(7, 5) **6.** F(4, 5)

7. G(9, 2) **8.** H(7, 2)

9. J(4, 2) **10.** K(6, 5)

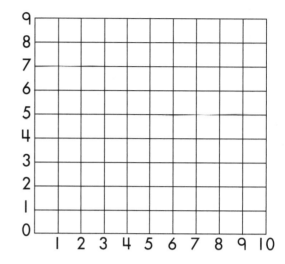

11. Connect the points to form a plane figure.
What figure did you draw? _____

12. Which points represent the vertices of the plane figure? _____

13. What is the length of the top base of the figure? _____

14. What is the length of the bottom base of the figure? _____

THINK

What is the shortest distance, in units, from the top base to the bottom base?
Explain how you found your answer.

0-7424-2985-7 *Using the Standards: Geometry*

Name_____ Date _____

Name Ordered Pairs

Directions: Give the coordinates of each point on the grid below.

1. A _____
2. B _____
3. C _____
4. D _____
5. E _____
6. F _____
7. G _____
8. H _____
9. I _____
10. J _____

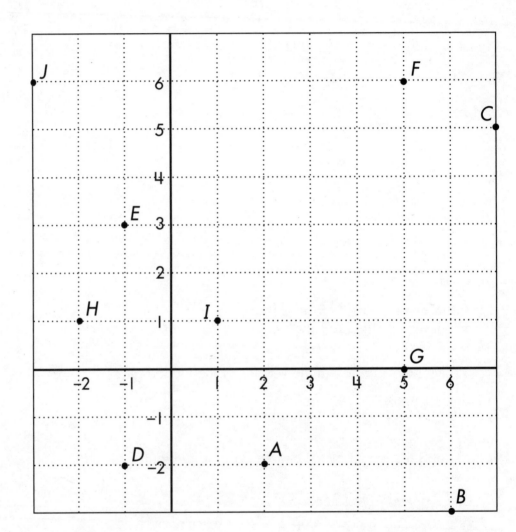

THINK

Name two line segments that are parallel to each other.

Name two line segments that intersect and are perpendicular to each other.

Name_____ Date _____

Endpoints of Line Segments

Directions: Use the grid below to help you answer each question.

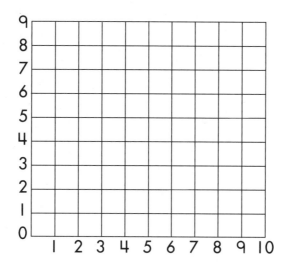

1. Line segment *AB* has endpoints at *A*(3, 2) and *B*(9, 2).
   What are the coordinates of the midpoint of line segment *AB*?   _____

2. Line segment *MN* has endpoints at *M*(4, 1) and *N*(4, 7).
   Line segment *RS* is the same length as line segment *MN*.
   The two segments are parallel to each other and have the same *y*-coordinates.
   Line segment *RS* is 5 units to the right of line segment *MN*.
   Name the coordinates of endpoints *R* and *S*.   _____

3. Line segment *CD* has endpoints at *C*(2, 5) and *D*(8, 5).
   Line segment *GH* is the perpendicular bisector of line segment *CD*.
   Line segment *CD* is the perpendicular bisector of line segment *GH*.
   Line segment *GH* is the same length as line segment *CD*.
   Name the coordinates of endpoints *G* and *H*.   _____

4. Isosceles triangle *ABC* has two vertices at *A*(4, 7) and *B*(2, 1).
   The base of the triangle is parallel to the *x*-axis.
   Name the coordinates of the other endpoint of the base, *C*.   _____

0-7424-2985-7 *Using the Standards: Geometry*

Name_____ Date _____

Scrambled Directions

Directions: Help Miguel! He dropped the directions on how to get from Seaside to Groveport. He still has his map, but the directions are scrambled. Using the map as a reference, help put Miguel's directions in the correct order. Number the steps from 1–10.

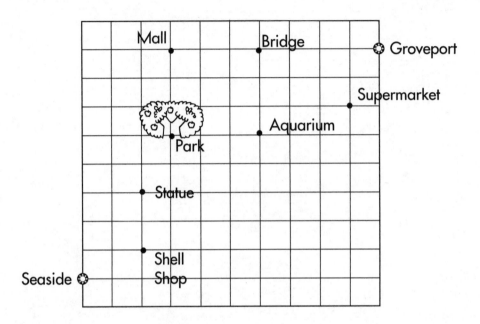

_____ Groveport is 2 blocks north and 1 block east from the supermarket.

_____ From the aquarium go 3 blocks east, then north to the supermarket.

_____ Leave Seaside and drive east 2 blocks, then north to the Shell Shop.

_____ Go east one block and north to the park.

_____ From the Shell Shop drive north past the statue.

_____ From the mall go east across the bridge.

_____ Go south to the aquarium.

_____ Go north to the mall.

0-7424-2985-7 *Using the Standards: Geometry*

Name_____ Date _____

Driving Directions

Directions: Use the grid and the compass rose to give each direction.
Travel is only possible along the grid lines.

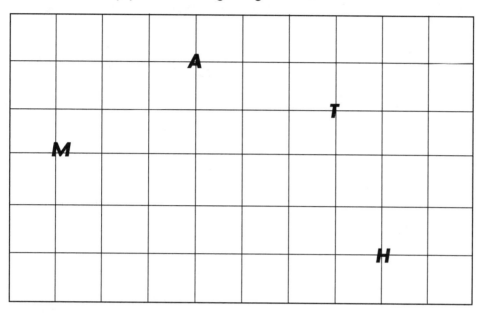

1. Michael is at location A. He needs to go to location M, then location T, and then back to location A.
   What distance does Michael travel? _____

   Directions: _____

   _____

2. Julia is at location H. She needs to go to location T, then location M. She then needs to return to location H before going on to location A.
   What distance does Julia travel? _____

   Directions: _____

   _____

3. Craig is at location M. He needs to go to location A after going to location T.
   How should he go?

   _____

55

0-7424-2985-7 *Using the Standards: Geometry*

Name_____ Date _____

Investigation Location

Directions: Create a secret code that can be revealed using the board below. Make a list of the squares that should be colored to reveal the message. Have a friend investigate and reveal your message.

	A	B	C	D	E	F	G	H	I	J	K
1											
2											
3											
4											
5											
6											
7											
8											
9											
10											
11											
12											
13											
14											
15											
16											
17											

0-7424-2985-7 *Using the Standards: Geometry*

Name_____ Date _____

Dot-to-Dot Drawing

Directions: Plot each ordered pair. Then connect the dots in the order that they are listed to complete the picture.

| (5, 8) | (6, 7) | (7, 5) | $(7\frac{1}{2}, 2)$ | (5, 2) | (5, 5) | (5, 8) |

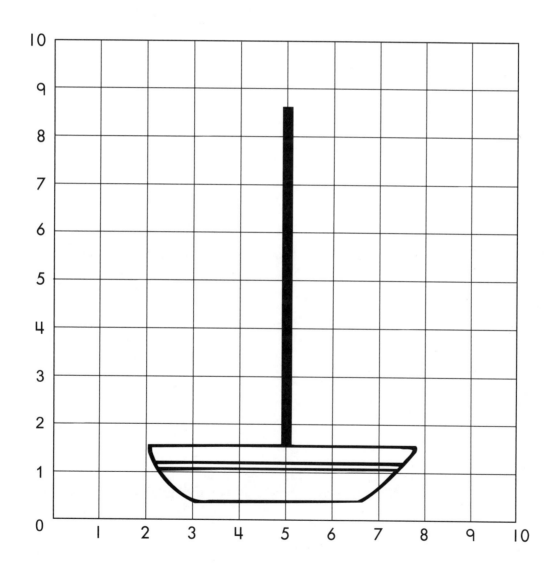

0-7424-2985-7 *Using the Standards: Geometry*

Name_____ Date _____

Drawing Lines of Symmetry

A **line of symmetry** is a line that divides a picture or shape into two equal halves. Each half is a mirror image of the other half. A line of symmetry can be vertical, horizontal, or diagonal.

A square has 4 lines of symmetry.

Directions: Draw each figure described.

1. a letter with a horizontal line of symmetry

2. a letter with a vertical line of symmetry

3. a figure with at least 4 lines of symmetry

4. a figure with at least 8 lines of symmetry

THINK

Do all regular polygons have at least 1 line of symmetry? Explain.

0-7424-2985-7 *Using the Standards: Geometry*

Name_____ Date _____

Create a Symmetrical Drawing

Directions: The left side of a picture is shown. The dashed line is a line of symmetry Use the grid to draw the right side so that the picture is symmetrical.

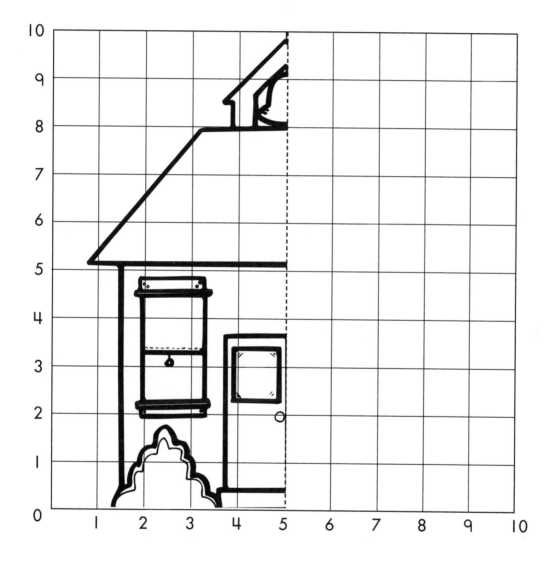

THINK

Describe how you decided where to draw on the right side of the picture.

Talk with a partner about the different ways to create the right half of the picture.

Does one way seem easier than another?

0-7424-2985-7 *Using the Standards: Geometry*

Name_____ Date _____

Plot the Punchline

Directions: Plot the ordered pairs on the graph in order to reveal the answer to the riddle.

What is the difference between Here and There?

Points to plot:

(4, 0)	(4, 4)	(2, 6)	(6, 6)	(4, 4)	(4, 1)
(4, 5)	(3, 6)	(5, 6)	(4, 2)	(4, 3)	

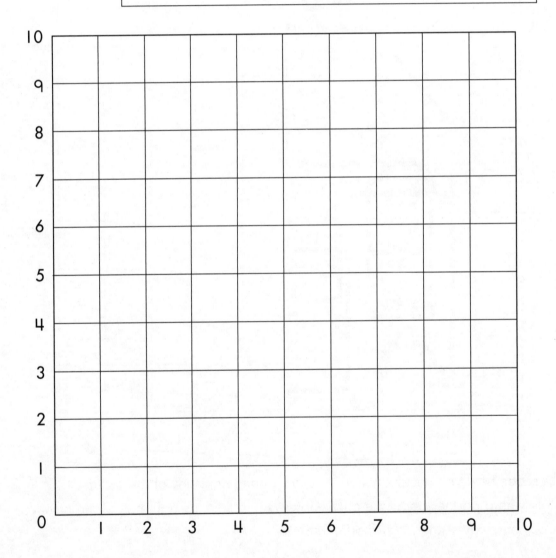

0-7424-2985-7 *Using the Standards: Geometry*

Name_____ Date _____

Flip Across a Line of Symmetry

A figure can be reflected or flipped over a line of symmetry so that the figure and its image are an equal distance from the line of symmetry.

The coordinate grid helps show that the figures are reflections of each other.

Directions: Name the ordered pairs of the image of the quadrilateral when it is reflected across the dashed line of symmetry.

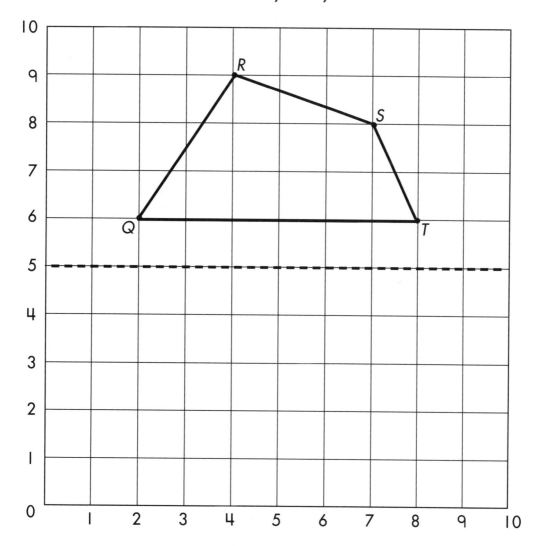

0-7424-2985-7 *Using the Standards: Geometry*

Name_____ Date _____

Create Your Own Problems

1. Write a question about the distance between two ordered pairs on a coordinate grid.

2. Draw a right triangle on a coordinate grid. Label the vertices with letters. Write a question that asks about the vertices or the lengths of the base.

3. Draw a coordinate grid map of your neighborhood. Locate familiar places on your coordinate grid. Write a question about the locations of the places on your map.

4. Write a question about a figure that has at least two lines of symmetry.

5. Use ordered pairs to create a dot-to-dot picture.

0-7424-2985-7 *Using the Standards: Geometry*

Name_____ Date _____

Check Your Skills

Use the coordinate grid below for questions 1 and 2.

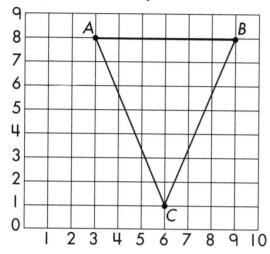

1. Name the coordinates of vertices A, B, and C.
    What type of triangle is ABC?   _____

2. What is the length of base $\overline{AB}$? Name the midpoint
    of base $\overline{AB}$ on the coordinate grid.   _____

3. Graph the ordered pairs (2, 6), (8, 6), (7, 2), and (1, 2).
    Connect the points with line segments.
    What is the name of the plane figure that you created?

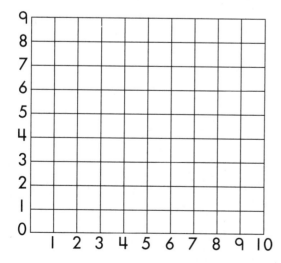

                                                    _____

0-7424-2985-7 *Using the Standards: Geometry*

Name_____ Date _____

Check Your Skills (cont.)

Use the grid to answer questions 4 – 7.

Miguel, Lisa, Holly, and James are playing hide-and-seek.
Their locations (labeled with their initials) are shown on the coordinate grid.

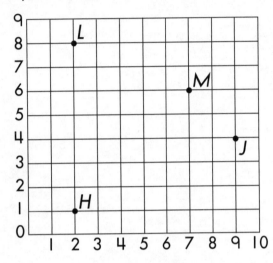

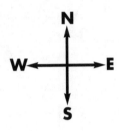

4. Which person is the farthest east? _____

5. Who is located to the north of Miguel's position?
What are the coordinates of this player? _____

6. What is the distance, in units, between Holly and Lisa? _____

7. What directions should James follow to locate Lisa's position? _____

8. Describe how to plot each point on a coordinate.
Assume you are starting at (0, 0).

a. (3, 5) _____

b. (–1, –4) _____

0-7424-2985-7 *Using the Standards: Geometry*

Name_____ Date _____

Flips, Slides, and Turns

A **flip** is a transformation that creates a mirror image of the original image. A horizontal flip is a flip across a vertical line. A vertical flip is a flip across a horizontal line.

horizontal flip

vertical flip

A **slide** is a transformation that creates an image moved from the location of the original image. A slide can move in any direction.

A **turn** is a transformation that creates a rotated image of the original image. A turn can be clockwise or counterclockwise.

Directions: Name the transformation that was performed on each letter tile.

1.

_____

2.

_____

3.

_____

4.

_____

5.

_____

6.

_____

0-7424-2985-7 *Using the Standards: Geometry*

Name_____ Date _____

Initial Transformation

Directions: Write the initials of your name in block capital letters. Then perform each transformation.

A B C D E F G
H I J K L M N
O P Q R S T U
V W X Y Z

I. flip over a horizontal line

2. 180° turn

3. flip over a vertical line

4. slide to the right

THINK

Is there a capital letter that looks the same under a flip, a slide, and a turn?

0-7424-2985-7 *Using the Standards: Geometry*

Name_____ Date _____

Congruent Figures

Congruent figures have the same size and shape.

Directions: Draw each transformation in the space provided.

1. flip over a vertical line

2. 90° turn counterclockwise

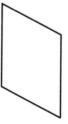

3. slide down and right

THINK

When a figure undergoes a slide, a flip, or a turn, the transformed

image is _____ to the original figure.

0-7424-2985-7 *Using the Standards: Geometry*

Name_____ Date _____

Flip to the Finish Line

Directions: Create a maze so that you can get from START to FINISH by following a
path of horizontal and vertical flips. Each move is left, right, up, or down.
The path has been started for you. Trade mazes with a partner and see
if you can solve each other's puzzle.

START

FINISH

0-7424-2985-7 *Using the Standards: Geometry*

Name_____ Date _____

Transforming Words

Directions: Show the word with each letter transformed as stated.

1. # SHAPE _____ _____ _____ _____ _____

   horizontal flip

2. # MATH _____ _____ _____ _____

   180° turn

3. # THREE _____ _____ _____ _____ _____

   vertical flip

4. # CUBE _____ _____ _____ _____

   slide

DO MORE

Choose a transformation, and write each letter of your school's name.

0-7424-2985-7 *Using the Standards: Geometry*

Name_____ Date _____

Multiple Transformations

Directions: Perform the indicated transformations.

1. Flip the figure horizontally. Then flip the resulting image vertically.

2. Flip the figure vertically. Then flip the resulting image horizontally.

3. Turn the image 180°.

THINK

Flipping a figure horizontally then vertically, or vertically then horizontally,

has the same effect as _____.

Draw more figures to test your hypothesis.

0-7424-2985-7 *Using the Standards: Geometry*

Name_____ Date _____

Transformation Match-Up

Directions: Match each letter with the appropriate transformation of the letter R. Not all transformations will be used.

1. ____

a. a slide

2. ____

b. a horizontal flip

c. a 180° turn

3. ____

d. a vertical flip

e. a 90° turn counterclockwise

4. ____

f. a 90° turn clockwise

5. ____

DO MORE

Which transformation was not used? Draw it in the space to the right.

0-7424-2985-7 *Using the Standards: Geometry*

Name_____ Date _____

Drawing Congruent Figures

Directions: Create three congruent figures by drawing each transformation.
Use the original figure for each transformation.

	Slide	**Vertical Flip**	**Counterclockwise Turn**
1.	_____	_____	_____
2.	_____	_____	_____
3.	_____	_____	_____
4.	_____	_____	_____
5.	_____	_____	_____

0-7424-2985-7 *Using the Standards: Geometry*

Name_____ Date _____

Designing with Transformations

Directions: Begin with the right triangle. Tell what transformations are needed to create the finished design. Draw each step of the process.

Step 1

Step 2   _____

Step 3   _____

Step 4 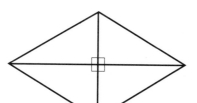   _____

THINK

 What is the name of the plane figure in Step 4?

0-7424-2985-7 *Using the Standards: Geometry*

Name_____ Date _____

Lines of Symmetry

Directions: Draw all lines of symmetry for each figure.
Tell how many lines of symmetry you drew.

1.

_____

2.

_____

3.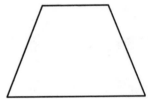

_____

4.

_____

5.

_____

6.

_____

THINK

How many lines of symmetry does a circle have? Can you draw them all?

0-7424-2985-7 *Using the Standards: Geometry*

Name_____ Date _____

A Symmetry Riddle

Directions: Follow the clues to solve the riddle. Use uppercase letters.

Riddle: I'm "round" on the outside and "high" in the middle. What state am I?

A B C D E F G

H I J K L M N

O P Q R S T U

V W X Y Z

I have 4 letters in my name.

My first and last letters have an infinite number of lines of symmetry.

My second and third letters have two lines of symmetry.

What state am I?

____ ____ ____ ____

0-7424-2985-7 *Using the Standards: Geometry*

Name_____ Date _____

Point Symmetry

A figure that is turned about a point and looks exactly like itself before one complete rotation (360 degrees) has **point symmetry**.

Point symmetry is also called **rotational symmetry**.

Directions: Decide if each figure has point symmetry. Write yes or no.

1.

_____

2.

_____

3.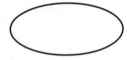

_____

4.

_____

5.

_____

6.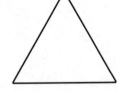

_____

0-7424-2985-7 *Using the Standards: Geometry*

Name_____ Date _____

Rotating About a Point

Directions: Draw each picture after it is turned one-quarter turn (90°) clockwise about the point shown.

1.

•

2.

•

0-7424-2985-7 *Using the Standards: Geometry*

Name_____ Date _____

Real World Transformations

Directions: Think about each object as it is used in the real world. Often when objects are used, they are placed in a different position. For each object, circle each transformation which you might see the object while it is being used.

1.    flip   slide   turn

2. 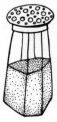   flip   slide   turn

3.    flip   slide   turn

4.    flip   slide   turn

DO MORE

     Choose one object shown above and explain how it is used in its transformed state.

0-7424-2985-7 *Using the Standards: Geometry*

Name_____ Date _____

Create Your Own Problems

1. Identify an object around your house or school that you can use in its normal position and in a transformed position. Write a problem about the object.

2. Make a drawing using transformations of a rectangle. Exchange drawings with a partner and see if you can determine which transformations were used by the other person.

3. Write a word problem about how a slide transformation might be used in a board game.

4. Write a question about how many lines of symmetry are in specific letters or words.

5. Draw a plane figure that has at least two lines of symmetry. Write a question about the figure.

0-7424-2985-7 *Using the Standards: Geometry*

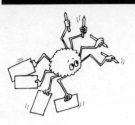

Name_____ Date _____

Check Your Skills

1. Name a letter of the alphabet that has rotational symmetry.

_____

2. How many lines of symmetry does a regular pentagon have?

_____

3. Which transformation has the same effect as reflecting a figure vertically, and then horizontally?

_____

4. Which transformation is shown at the right?

_____

5. What is the next figure in the pattern of transformations?

      _____

0-7424-2985-7 *Using the Standards: Geometry*

Name_____ Date _____

Check Your Skills (cont.)

6. Sketch the figure below after a flip across the dashed segment.

7. How many lines of symmetry does the figure have? Draw the lines.

_____

8. Circle the figures that have point (rotational) symmetry.

9. Describe what letter is formed when the transformation described is applied.

    a. The letter "W" is flipped vertically. _____

    b. The letter "d" is turned one-half turn clockwise. _____

10. Name the transformation that can be applied to 99 to get a result that resembles each.

    a. two uppercase P letters _____

    b. two lowercase d letters _____

    c. two number sixes _____

81

I See It, Do You?

Directions: Play a variation of "I See Something You Don't See" but use objects that model 3-dimensional solid figures instead of colors.

The rules:

• Three people play in a small group.

• The shape must be in the room where you are playing.

• One player selects an object in the room that models a solid figure.

• The player names a solid figure as the clue.

> For example, a player says: I see an object that you don't see, and it is shaped like a cylinder.

• The other two players take turns making guesses about the secret object that models the solid figure.

• The player that identifies the object first, gets to select the next object and give the clue.

• If no players guess correctly after a specified amount of time, then the clue-giving player gets another turn at selecting the object and giving the clue.

• Here is a list of solid figures that objects can model.

cube	cylinder
rectangular prism	square pyramid
cone	sphere
triangular prism	triangular pyramid

0-7424-2985-7 *Using the Standards: Geometry*

Name_____ Date _____

Dot Paper Drawing

Directions: Use the dot paper to draw each figure.

1. a right triangle with a base of 2 units and a height of 5 units

2. a rectangle that is 4 units by 3 units

3. a parallelogram that has no right angles, a base of 4 units, and a height of 2 units

0-7424-2985-7 *Using the Standards: Geometry*

Name_____ Date _____

Isosceles Drawings

Directions: Use the dot paper to draw each figure.

1. an isosceles triangle with a base of 10 units and a height of 6 units

2. a line segment that divides the triangle from question 1 into an isosceles trapezoid and a smaller isosceles triangle

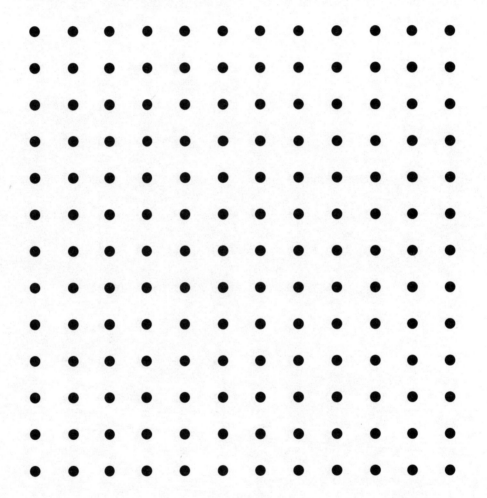

THINK

Explain how you know that the line segment you drew divides the larger isosceles triangle into an isosceles trapezoid and a smaller isosceles triangle.

0-7424-2985-7 *Using the Standards: Geometry*

Name_____ Date _____

Sizing a Triangle

Directions: Use a ruler to measure the sides of each triangle, and study the angles. Name each triangle with all the names that apply from the following list.

scalene	isosceles	equilateral
right	acute	obtuse

1.

_____

2.

_____

3.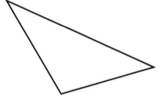

_____

4.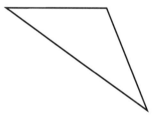

_____

5.

_____

6.

_____

DO MORE

Which words in the list name a triangle based on its sides?

Which words name a triangle based on its angles?

0-7424-2985-7 *Using the Standards: Geometry*

Name_____ Date _____

Classify Quadrilaterals

Directions: Give all names for each quadrilateral shown. Not all names will be used for each shape.

rectangle	parallelogram	square
rhombus	trapezoid	

1. _____

2. _____

3. _____

4. _____

0-7424-2985-7 *Using the Standards: Geometry*

Name_____ Date _____

Solid Figures in the Real World

Directions: Think about what each solid figure named below looks like. List items you use in your life that model each solid figure.

1. cone _____

_____

2. cylinder _____

_____

3. cube _____

_____

4. sphere _____

_____

5. rectangular prism _____

6. triangular prism _____

7. square pyramid _____

8. triangular pyramid _____

THINK

Which solid figures are more commonly used in your life?

Name_____ Date _____

Create a Rectangular Prism

Directions: Follow the steps to draw a rectangular prism.

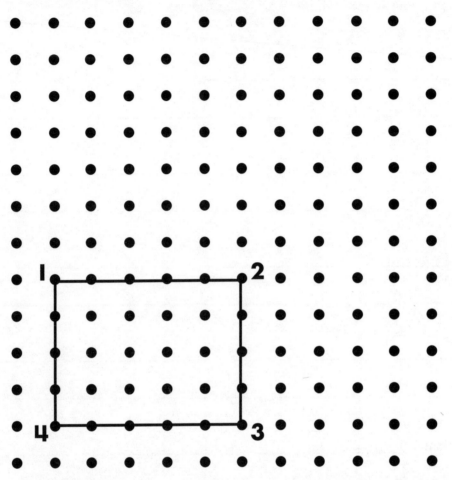

Step 1: Draw a rectangle with vertices 1, 2, 3, and 4. This step has been completed for you.

Step 2: Draw a congruent rectangle in the upper right portion of the dot paper. Label the vertices 5, 6, 7, and 8 to correspond to vertices 1, 2, 3, and 4.

Step 3: Connect vertices 1 and 5, 2 and 6, and 3 and 7 with solid line segments.

Step 4: Connect vertices 4 and 8 with a dashed line segment.

Step 5: What edges drawn in previous steps should be made with dashed line segments? Adjust your drawing.

0-7424-2985-7 *Using the Standards: Geometry*

Create a Square Pyramid

Directions: Follow the steps, and learn how to draw a square pyramid.

• 5

1 •   • 4

2 •   • 3

Use solid line segment for Steps 1 – 3.

    Step 1: Connect dots 1 to 2, 2 to 3, and 3 to 4.

    Step 2: Connect dots 5 to 1 and 5 to 4.

    Step 3: Connect dots 5 to 2 and 5 to 3.

Use a dashed line segment for Step 4.

    Step 4: Connect dots 1 to 4.

DO MORE

Write instructions on how to draw a triangular pyramid.

0-7424-2985-7 *Using the Standards: Geometry*

Name_____ Date _____

Create a Triangular Prism

Directions: Follow the steps to draw a triangular prism.

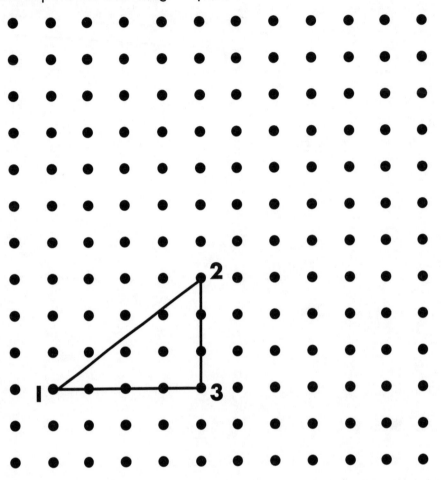

Step 1: Draw a triangle with vertices 1, 2, and 3. This step has been completed for you.

Step 2: Draw a congruent triangle in the upper right portion of the dot paper. Label the vertices 4, 5, and 6 to correspond to vertices 1, 2, and 3.

Step 3: Connect vertices 1 and 4, 2 and 5, and 3 and 6. Use solid line segments if you would be able to see them. If an edge should be hidden from view, use a dashed line segment.

0-7424-2985-7 *Using the Standards: Geometry*

Faces of a Solid Figure

Directions: For each of the following, identify the solid figure that has the number and type of each face given. Draw the solid figure in the space provided.

1.

4 faces

2 faces

2.

2 faces

1 side (flattened)

3.

6 faces

4.

1 face

4 faces

0-7424-2985-7 *Using the Standards: Geometry*

Name_____ Date _____

Making a Rectangular Prism

The **net** of a solid figure is a 2-dimensional drawing of the faces
of a 3-dimensional solid figure. When the drawing is folded
on its dotted lines, the solid figure is formed.

Directions: Cut out the net below. Fold on the dotted line segments shown.
Tape the edges to form a rectangular prism.

rectangular prism

fold

fold

fold

fold

fold

92

Name_____ Date _____

Making a Cylinder

Directions: Cut out the net below. Make a cylinder.

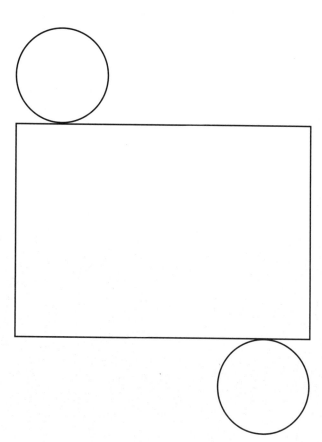

cylinder

THINK

Draw the net of a triangular prism in the space below.

0-7424-2985-7 *Using the Standards: Geometry*

Name_____ Date _____

Match Solid Figures to Nets

Directions: Tell what solid will be formed when each net is folded. Sketch each solid.

1.

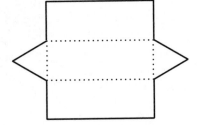

_____

2.

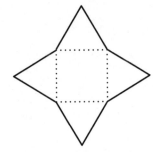

_____

3.

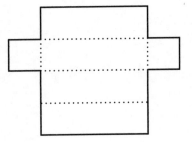

_____

4.

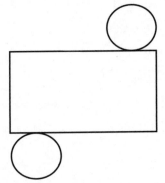

_____

Name_____ Date _____

Name That Solid Figure

Directions: Name a solid figure that matches each description.

1. a solid figure with one circular base

_____

2. a solid figure that has a rectangular base, but no other rectangular faces

_____

3. a solid figure with 6 vertices and two triangular bases

_____

4. a solid figure that has three triangular faces

_____

5. a solid figure that has no vertices and no flat faces

_____

0-7424-2985-7 *Using the Standards: Geometry*

Finding Perimeter

Perimeter is the distance around a figure. To find the perimeter of a plane figure, add the lengths of its sides. Perimeters are measured in linear units.

The perimeter of a rectangle can be found using the formula $P = 2l + 2w$.

Directions: Find the perimeter of each figure.

1.

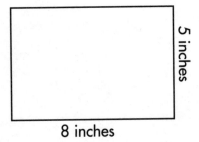

5 inches

8 inches

_____

2.

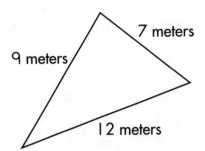

7 meters

9 meters

12 meters

_____

3.

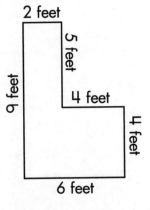

2 feet

5 feet

9 feet

4 feet

4 feet

6 feet

_____

4.

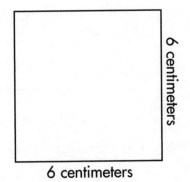

6 centimeters

6 centimeters

_____

0-7424-2985-7 *Using the Standards: Geometry*

Name_____ Date _____

Perimeter Designs

Directions: On the dot paper below, sketch a shape that has the given characteristics.

1. Figure *G* is a non-regular hexagon with a perimeter of 20 units.

2. Figure *H* is a rectangle with a perimeter of more than 12 units.

0-7424-2985-7 *Using the Standards: Geometry*

Name_____ Date _____

Virginia's Vegetable Garden

Directions: Solve the problem.

Virginia planted a vegetable garden in her yard next to her house. She chose this corner because the area gets a lot of morning sun, but does not get the hot afternoon sun. She wants to put a low fence around her garden so that her children and pets will stay out. How many yards of fencing does she need?

_____ yards

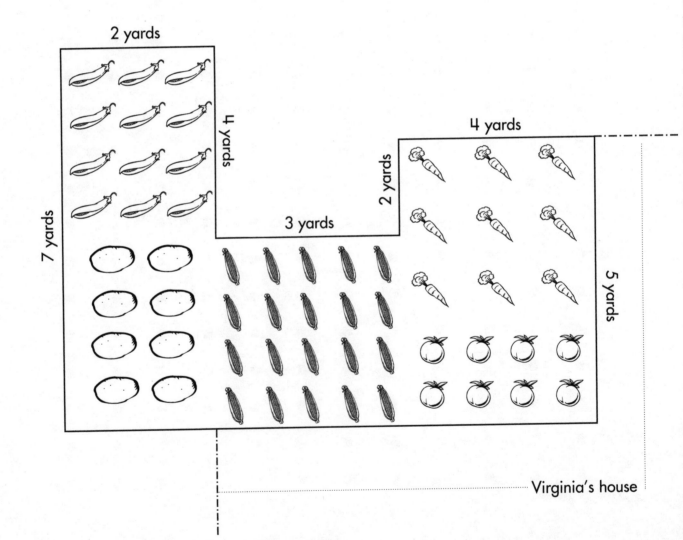

0-7424-2985-7 *Using the Standards: Geometry*

Name_____ Date _____

Finding Area

Area is the number of square units in the interior region of a plane figure.

The area of a rectangle can be found using the formula $A = lw$.

Directions: Find the area of each shape.

1.

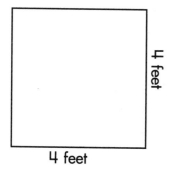

4 feet

4 feet

_____

2.

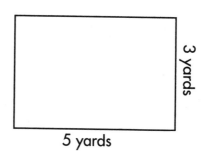

3 yards

5 yards

_____

3.

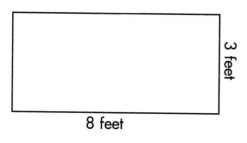

3 feet

8 feet

_____

4.

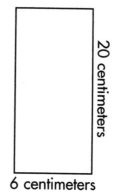

20 centimeters

6 centimeters

_____

0-7424-2985-7 *Using the Standards: Geometry*

Name_____ Date _____

Area Designs

Directions: On the dot paper below, sketch a shape that has the given characteristics.

1. Figure Q is an octagon with an area of 18 square units.

2. Figure P is a polygon with an area of 11 square units.

0-7424-2985-7 *Using the Standards: Geometry*

Name_____ Date _____

A Remodeling Problem

Directions: Solve the problem.

Carlos is refinishing his basement, and he wants to have new carpet installed. The basement has the dimensions shown below. How many square yards of carpet does Carlos need to completely cover the floor?
(Hint: Break the room up into smaller rectangles.)

_____ square yards

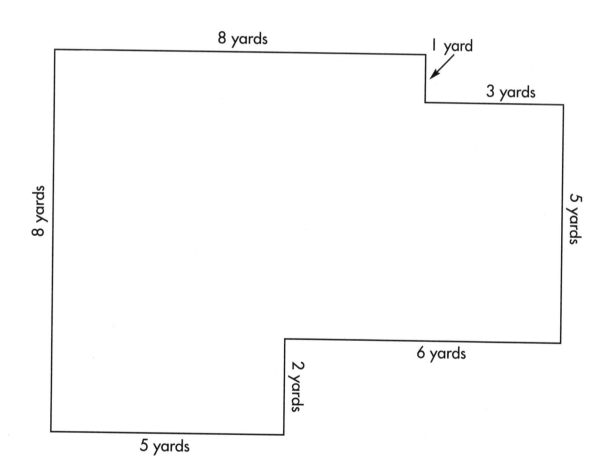

0-7424-2985-7 *Using the Standards: Geometry*

Name_____ Date _____

Which Formula?

Directions: Read each situation. Decide if the problem should be solved by finding an area or a perimeter. Circle the appropriate answer choice.

1. Alfonso is cutting a border to go around his fish tank. How much border does he need?

$P = 2l + 2w$ $A = lw$

2. Heather is mowing her parents' backyard. How much lawn does she mow?

$P = 2l + 2w$ $A = lw$

3. Mr. Mead is installing tile flooring in his bathroom. How many square feet of tile does he need?

$P = 2l + 2w$ $A = lw$

4. Chris is hanging wallpaper in his bedroom. How much wallpaper does he need?

$P = 2l + 2w$ $A = lw$

5. Donna is gluing a border around a portrait. How many inches of border does she need?

$P = 2l + 2w$ $A = lw$

6. Mr. Andrews is painting his garage walls. How much area does he need to cover with paint?

$P = 2l + 2w$ $A = lw$

7. Tina is hanging lights around her front window. How many feet of lights does she need?

$P = 2l + 2w$ $A = lw$

DO MORE

Choose one of the situations in questions 1–7 and explain how you decided on the formula.

0-7424-2985-7 *Using the Standards: Geometry*

Surface Area of Rectangular Prisms

The **surface area** of a rectangular prism is the sum of the areas of all its faces. Surface area is measured in square units.

If a prism has length *l*, width *w*, and height *h*, the formula $SA = 2lw + 2wh + 2lh$ can be used.

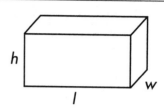

Directions: Find the surface area of each rectangular prism.

1.

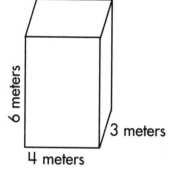

6 meters
3 meters
4 meters

_____

2.

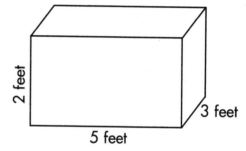

2 feet
3 feet
5 feet

_____

THINK

What is special about the length, width, and height of a cube?

Write a formula for the surface area of a cube.

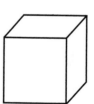

0-7424-2985-7 *Using the Standards: Geometry*

Name_____ Date _____

Volume of Rectangular Prisms

The **volume** of a rectangular prism is a measure of the space inside the figure. Volume is measured in cubic units.

A prism with length *l*, width *w*, and height *h*, has a volume of *V* = *lwh*.

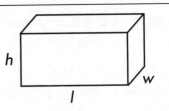

Directions: Find the volume of each rectangular prism.

1.

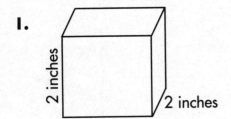

2 inches
2 inches
2 inches

_____

2.

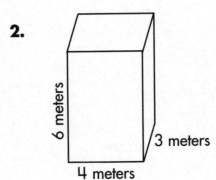

6 meters
3 meters
4 meters

_____

3.

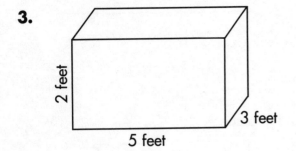

2 feet
5 feet
3 feet

_____

4.

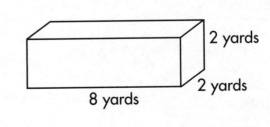

2 yards
2 yards
8 yards

_____

0-7424-2985-7 *Using the Standards: Geometry*

Name_____ Date _____

Surface Area or Volume?

Directions: Read each situation. Decide if the problem should be solved by finding surface area or volume. Circle the appropriate answer choice.

1. Hal is wrapping a birthday gift. How much wrapping paper is needed?   SA   V

2. Mr. Thomas is baking brownies. How much batter is needed?   SA   V

3. A manufacturer is printing labels for soup cans. How much paper is needed for each label?   SA   V

4. Carl is filling a saltwater aquarium. How much water does he need?   SA   V

5. Mrs. O'Brien's kids store their toys in a large bin. How many toys fit in the toy bin?   SA   V

6. Colleen is packing up books in a box. How many books fit in each box?   SA   V

7. Mr. Matthews is painting his house. How much paint does he need?   SA   V

8. Kerry is designing a new shoe box. How much cardboard does she need?   SA   V

9. Nancy is drying clothes. How many shirts will fit inside the dryer?   SA   V

10. Eddie drank 3 cans of juice yesterday. How much juice did he drink?   SA   V

DO MORE

Write a situation that can be solved by finding the surface area of a figure.

Then write a situation that can be solved by finding the volume of a figure.

0-7424-2985-7 *Using the Standards: Geometry*

Create Your Own Problems

1. Write a question about the perimeter of a regular polygon.

2. Write a word problem that involves finding the volume of a rectangular prism.

3. Write a problem that involves finding the surface area of a cube.

4. Write a question about a solid figure that has a circular base.

5. Write a word problem that must be solved by finding the area or perimeter of a figure.

Published by Instructional Fair. Copyright protected.

0-7424-2985-7 *Using the Standards: Geometry*

Name_____ Date _____

Check Your Skills

1. Which plane figure is modeled by a yield sign?

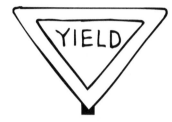

_____

2. The face of a cube has an area of 4 square meters.

What is the surface area of the cube? _____

3. Name two solid figures that have at least one circle as a face.

_____   _____

4. What solid figure is modeled by a ball of yarn?

_____

5. What shape has 2 acute angles, 2 obtuse angles, and only one set of parallel sides? Sketch the shape in the space below.

_____

0-7424-2985-7 *Using the Standards: Geometry*

Name_____ Date _____

Check Your Skills (cont.)

6. A rectangle has an area of 30 square meters. The length of the rectangle is 10 meters. What is the width?

_____

7. A stop sign is shaped like a regular octagon. The length of one side is 5 inches. What is the perimeter of the stop sign?

_____

8. Draw a net for a triangular prism.

9. What solid figure is modeled by the sand box?

6 feet

1 foot

8 feet

_____

10. How many cubic feet of sand will fit in the sand box?

_____

0-7424-2985-7 *Using the Standards: Geometry*

Post Test

1. Draw a set of parallel lines and line perpendicular to both.

2. What is the name of the plane figure below?

_____

3. Name a solid figure that has 6 vertices and 9 edges.

_____

4. Name the ordered pairs for each vertex of the shape shown.

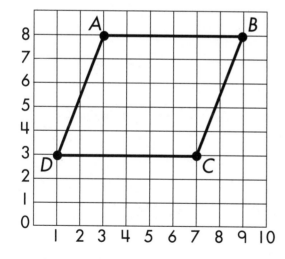

A _____

B _____

C _____

D _____

5. What is the length, in units, of base *AB* shown above? _____

0-7424-2985-7 *Using the Standards: Geometry*

Post Test (cont.)

6. How many lines of symmetry does the plane figure at the right have?

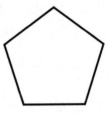

_____

7. What transformation is shown?

_____

8. Are the shapes below similar? Write yes or no.

 4 meters

4 meters

 5 meters

5 meters

_____

9. What is the volume of a box that has dimensions 5 inches by 9 inches by 3 inches?

_____

10. What is the surface area of the figure to the right?

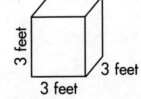

3 feet

3 feet

3 feet

_____

110

0-7424-2985-7 *Using the Standards: Geometry*

Answer Key

Pretest 7-8
1. Drawings will vary.
   Possible drawing is shown.
2.
3. Figure B
4. *D*(5, 8)
   E(2, 2)
   F(8, 2)
5. isosceles
6. 4;
7. 7 units
8. flip
9. 6; 12; 8

Segments, Rays, and Lines 9
Checks students' drawings. Sample drawings are shown.
1.
2.
3.
4.

THINK: no; A line cannot be drawn to a specific length because a line continues in both directions forever. A line segment can be drawn 4 inches long.

Classify Lines 10
Drawings will vary. Sample drawings are shown.
1.   2.
3.   4.

THINK: line *a* is parallel to line *c*. Drawings will vary. Sample drawings is shown.

Classify and Measure Angles 11
1. obtuse, 128°   2. right, 90°
3. acute, 50°   4. right, 90°
5. obtuse, 115°   6. acute, 50°
THINK: 180°

Modeling with Lines .12
1. perpendicular   2. parallel
3. intersecting   4. intersecting

Finding Angles in Numbers 13
Answers will vary.

Seeing Geometry in Words 14
1. 8   2. 5
3. TATE   4. 3
5. 5
DO MORE: Answers will vary.

Angles on a Clock Face 15
Answers will vary. Sample answers are shown.
1.
2.
3.

THINK: 6:00

Identify Polygons 16
1. yes   2. yes
3. yes   4. yes
5. no; A circle has 0 sides.
6. no; It is not a closed figure.
THINK: Answers will vary.

Draw Quadrilaterals .17
Drawings will vary. Sample drawings are shown.
1.   2.
3.   4.
5.   6.

THINK: True. A square is a rectangle because it has 4 right angles and 2 pairs of parallel sides.

111

Answer Key

Plane Figures 18
Drawings will vary. Sample drawings are shown.

1. 3;
2. 4;
3. 5;
4. 6;
5. 8;

Regular Polygons 19
1. regular
2. irregular; All the sides are not of equal length.
3. regular
4. regular
5. irregular; All the sides are not of equal length.
6. regular

THINK: No. All squares have 4 sides of equal length.

Sides and Vertices 20
1. 5; 5
2. 0; 0
3. 8; 8
4. 3; 3
5. 6; 6
6. 4; 4

THINK: 7; The number of sides is the same as the number of vertices in any polygon.

Plane Figures in Drawings 21
Answers will vary. Sample answers are given.
1. Blanket is a square. Diaper tabs are quadrilaterals.
2. The tub, mirror, and rug are made of rectangles. The shower head is a trapezoid. The lights above the mirror, and knob on the mirror are circles.
3. Clock face and the center of the clock are circles. The front of the clock and the side of the clock are trapezoids. The clock hands are triangles.
4. The stones are made of parallelograms, trapezoids, and triangles.

Polygon Puzzle 22

Polygon Puzzle, Part II 23

Types of Triangles 24
Drawings will vary. Sample drawings are shown to scale.

1.
2.
3.
4.

THINK: yes. An equilateral triangle has at least 2 sides of equal length.

Definitions of Plane Figures 25
1. parallel
2. scalene
3. right
4. equilateral
5. parallelogram
6. parallel

Sketch Triangles and Quadrilaterals 26
Drawings will vary. Sample drawings are shown.
1. equilateral triangle;
2. parallelogram;
3. isosceles triangle;
4. rhombus;

Properties of Quadrilaterals 27

parallelogram

a quadrilateral with 2 pairs of opposite sides that are parallel and equal in length

a parallelogram with 4 right angles

a parallelogram with 4 equal sides

rectangle

rhombus

a rectangle with 4 equal equals

square

DO MORE: 1. true; 2. false

0-7424-2985-7 *Using the Standards: Geometry*

Answer Key

Faces and Edges of Solid Figures 28

	Solid Figure	Number of Faces	Number of Edges	Number of Vertices	Shapes of Faces
1.	cube	6	12	8	squares
2.	triangular prism	5	9	6	rectangles triangles
3.	rectangular prism	6	12	8	rectangles
4.	rectangular pyramid	5	8	5	rectangle triangles
5.	triangular pyramid	4	6	4	triangles

Identify Solid Figures 29

1. Figures 3 and 5
2. Figure 2
3. Figures 1 and 3
4. Figures 4 and 5

Identify Solid Figures Around You 30

Answers will vary.

Identify Solid Figures Around You, Part II 31

Answers will vary.

Solid Figure Detective 32

1. cone
2. triangular prism
3. cylinder
4. triangular pyramid
5. cube

DO MORE: Answers will vary.

Stacking Solid Figures 33

Students' drawings will vary. Sample drawings are shown.
1. yes; Figure C has be to turned to stand on its triangular face and Figure J has to be on top.
2. no; Figures F and J have to be on top.
3. yes; Figure C has be to turned to stand on its triangular face and Figure D has to be on top.

THINK: Figure I because it has no faces. Figures D, F, and J have to be on top because each has only one base.

Follow the Path 34

Answers will vary. Sample answer is shown. (1. is shown with solid line. 2. is shown with dashed line)

Similar Figures 35

1. 3
2. 4
3. 5

Draw Shapes with Symmetry 36

THINK: Answers will vary, but A, B, C, D, E, H, I, K, M, O, T, U, V, W, X, and Y are often symmetrical.
Answers will vary depending on names.

Word Scramble 37

1. circle
2. solid
3. parallelogram
4. cone
5. symmetry
6. triangle
7. rhombus
8. prism
9. rectangle
10. square
11. pyramid
12. plane
13. vertex
14. cube
15. face
16. edge

   0-7424-2985-7 *Using the Standards: Geometry*

Answer Key

Scramble Word Search 38

```
P R I S M D P Y R A M I D X
A O I Q F Q M W F R S Y L A
R G H U E T F J L E S A Z R
A N V A W Q A H B C O N E H
L O P R T Y C F D T L K L U
L W G E D G E S J A I X V Y
E K R L T E W Y M N D L C I
L H H D F S A M B G U I U T
O Y O G P N A M P L N R B W
G F M C L K X E V E R T E X
R C B S A G K T L W F C S J
A M U R N G T R I A N G L E
M V S A E F T Y C I R C L E
```

Create Your Own Problems 39

Answers will vary.

Check Your Skills 40–41

1. Drawings will vary.
   Sample drawing is shown to scale.
2. All angles have equal measures.
   All sides are the same length.

3. triangular prism; It is a prism because the 2 triangular faces are the bases.
4. Drawings will vary. Sample drawing is shown to scale.

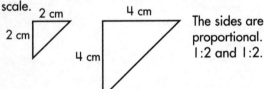

   The sides are proportional. 1:2 and 1:2.

5. 4; 6; 4
6. cube
7. 8
8. triangular prism, cylinder, cube, rectangular prism
9. cone
10. 2, 4, 5, 6, 7, 9

Around the Neighborhood 42

1. 5   2. 4
3. 5   4. beach and park

THINK: yes, up 3 blocks and right 2 blocks, or right 2 blocks and up 3 blocks.

Secret Hideout 43–44

1. D3   2. 3   3. B5
4. 7 meters
5. C11

Nuts About Newspapers 45–46

Results of the game will vary.

Drawing with Coordinates 47

1–2.
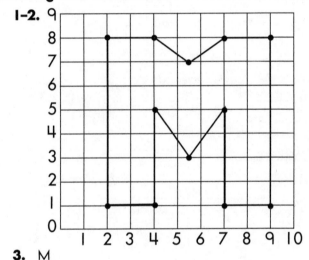

3. M

Draw a Solid Figure .48

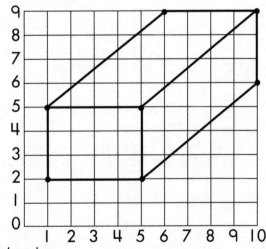

rectangular prism

0-7424-2985-7 *Using the Standards: Geometry*

Answer Key

Name the Vertices 49
1. A(4, 8); B(1, 2); C(8, 1)
2. R(2, −7); S(3, −1); T(8, −7)
3. L(4, 7); M(9, 7); N(7, 2); O(2, 1); P(1, 5)
4. H(−9, 5); I(−4, 8); J(−1, 1); K(−5, 5)

One Point Included 50
Graphs will vary. Sample graphs are shown.

1.

2.

Graphing Ordered Pairs 51
1–10.

11. trapezoid
12. B, E, F, G
13. 3 units
14. 8 units

THINK: 3, counted the units from point F to point J.

Name Ordered Pairs .52
1. (2, −2)
2. (6, −3)
3. (7, 5)
4. (−1, −2)
5. (−1, 3)
6. (5, 6)
7. (5, 0)
8. (−2, 1)
9. (1, 1)
10. (−3, 6)

THINK: Possible answers: DA and HI; JF and HI; JF and DA; FG and ED. HI and ED

Endpoints of Line Segments 53
1. (6, 2)
2. (9, 1) and (9, 7)
3. (5, 2) and (5, 8)
4. (6, 1)

Scrambled Directions .54
8 Groveport is 2 blocks north and 1 block east from the supermarket.

7 From the aquarium go 3 blocks east, then north to the supermarket.

1 Leave Seaside and drive east 2 blocks, then north to the Shell Shop.

3 Go east one block and north to the park.

2 From the Shell Shop drive north past the statue.

5 From the mall go east across the bridge.

6 Go south to the aquarium.

4 Go north to the mall.

0-7424-2985-7 *Using the Standards: Geometry*

Answer Key

Driving Directions

Directions will vary. Sample directions are given.
1. 16 units; 2 units south, 3 units west, 6 units east,
   1 unit north, 3 units west, 1 unit north
2. 28 units; 3 units north, 1 unit west, 6 units west,
   1 unit south, 7 units east, 2 units south, 4 units north,
   4 units west
3. 6 units east, 1 unit north, 3 units west, 1 unit north

Investigation Location

Secret codes and lists will vary.

Dot-to-Dot Drawing

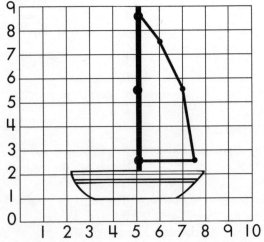

Drawing Lines of Symmetry

Drawings will vary. Sample drawings are shown.

1. E   2. H
3. □   4. ⬡

THINK: yes. A regular polygon has sides of equal lengths so the polygon will have a line of symmetry through the midpoints of opposite sides.

Create a Symmetry Drawing

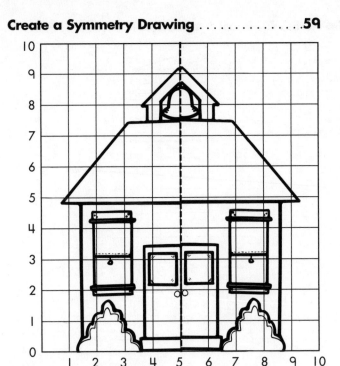

THINK: Descriptions and discussions will vary.

Plot the Punchline

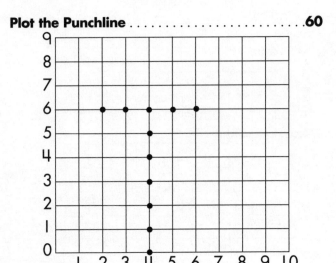

    0-7424-2985-7 *Using the Standards: Geometry*

Answer Key

Flip Across a Line of Symmetry 61

(2, 4), (4, 1), (7, 2), (8, 4)

Create Your Own Problems 62

Answers will vary.

Check Your Skills 63–64

1. A(3, 8), B(9, 8), C(6, 1); isosceles
2. 6 units; The midpoint is at (6, 8).
3. parallelogram
4. James
5. Lisa, (2, 8)
6. 7
7. 7 units left and 4 units up; or 4 units up and 7 units left
8. **a.** Move right 3 units, then up 5 units. Plot the point.
    b. Move left 1 unit, then down 4 units. Plot the point.

Flips, Slides, and Turns 65

1. slide
2. counterclockwise turn
3. horizontal flip
4. vertical flip
5. 180° turn
6. slide

Initial Transformation 66

Answers will vary. **THINK:** 0

Congruent Figures 67

THINK: congruent

Flip to the Finish Line 68

Answers will vary.

Transforming Words 69

1. SHAPE   2. MATH
3. THREE   4. CUBE

DO MORE: Answers will vary.

Multiple Transformations 70

DO MORE: turning 180°

Transformation Match-Up 71

1. e   2. b   3. d
4. a   5. f

DO MORE: a 180° turn **R**

Drawing Congruent Figures 72

0-7424-2985-7 *Using the Standards: Geometry*

Answer Key

Designing with Transformations **73**

Answers will vary. Sample answer is given.
Step 2: vertical flip upward
Step 3: horizontal flip to the left
Step 4: vertical flip downward
THINK: rhombus

Lines of Symmetry **74**

1. 4;

2. 6;

3. 1

4. 8

5. 5

6. 2

THINK: There are an infinite number of lines of symmetry for a circle. No.

A Symmetry Riddle **75**

OHIO

Rotating About a Point **76**

1. yes   **2.** yes
3. yes   **4.** yes
5. no   **6.** yes

Point Symmetry **77**

1.

2.

Real World Transformations **78**

1. flip, slide, turn   **2.** flip, slide, turn
3. flip, slide, turn   **4.** slide
DO MORE: Answers will vary.

Create Your Own Problems **79**

Answers will vary.

Check Your Skills **80–81**

1. Answers will vary. Sample answers: O and I
2. 5
3. turn
4. horizontal flip
5.

6.

7. 4;

8. All figures are circled except the first and fifth ones.
9. **a.** M
     b. P
10. **a.** horizontal flip
      b. vertical flip
      c. 180° turn

I See It, Do You? **82**

Students should play the game in groups of three.

Dot Paper Drawing **83**

1.–3.

Isosceles Drawings **84**

1.–2.

0-7424-2985-7 *Using the Standards: Geometry*

Answer Key

THINK: The line segment is placed to cross the midpoint of the height. Because the base angles are congruent and the sides are the same length, it is an isosceles trapezoid.

Sizing a Triangle 85

1. right, isosceles
2. acute, equilateral, isosceles
3. obtuse, scalene   **4.** obtuse, scalene
5. right, scalene   **6.** acute, scalene

THINK: The words that name a triangle by its sides are scalene, isosceles, and equilateral. The words that name a triangle by its angles are acute, obtuse, and right.

Classify Quadrilaterals 86

1. parallelogram, rectangle
2. parallelogram, rhombus
3. trapezoid
4. parallelogram, rectangle, rhombus, square

Solid Figures in the Real World 87

Answers will vary.
THINK: Answers will vary.

Create a Rectangular Prism 88

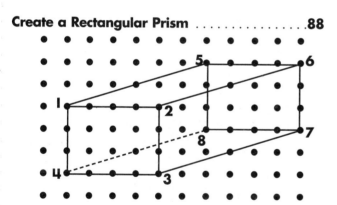

Edges 5 to 8 and 8 to 7 should be dashed line segments.

Create a Square Pyramid 89

DO MORE: Instructions will vary, but should include drawing a triangle and a point above it. Then connecting each vertex of the triangle that point.

Create a Triangular Prism 90

Faces of a Solid Figure 91

1. rectangular prism   **2.** cylinder

3. cube   **4.** square pyramid

Making a Rectangular Prism 92

Cut out, fold, and make the cube.

Making a Cylinder 93

Cut out, fold, and make the cylinder.
THINK:

Match Solid Figures to Nets 94

1. triangular prism   **2.** square pyramid
3. rectangular prism   **4.** cylinder

Name That Solid Figure 95

1. cone   **2.** rectangular pyramid
3. triangular prism   **4.** triangular pyramid
5. sphere

Finding Perimeter 96

1. 26 inches   **2.** 28 meters
3. 30 feet   **4.** 24 centimeters

0-7424-2985-7 *Using the Standards: Geometry*

Answer Key

Perimeter Designs 97

Drawings will vary. Sample drawings are shown.

1.-2.

Virginia's Vegetable Garden 98

24

Finding Area 99

1. 16 square feet
2. 15 square yards
3. 24 square feet
4. 120 square centimeters

Area Designs 100

Drawings will vary. Sample drawings are shown.

1.-2.

A Remodeling Problem 101

73

Which Formula? 102

1. $P = 2l + 2w$
2. $A = lw$
3. $A = lw$
4. $A = lw$
5. $P = 2l + 2w$
6. $A = lw$
7. $P = 2l + 2w$

DO MORE: Answers will vary.

Surface Area of Rectangular Prisms 103

1. 108 square meters
2. 62 square feet

THINK: The length, width, and height are all equal.
$V = 6s^2$

Volume of Rectangular Prisms 104

1. 8 cubic inches
2. 72 cubic meters
3. 30 cubic feet
4. 32 cubic yards

Surface Area or Volume? 105

1. SA
2. V
3. SA
4. V
5. V
6. V
7. SA
8. SA
9. V
10. V

DO MORE: Answers will vary.

Create Your Own Problems 106

Answers will vary.

Check Your Skills 107–108

1. triangle
2. 24 square meters
3. cone, cylinder
4. sphere
5. trapezoid
6. 3 meters

7. 40 inches
8.
9. rectangular prism
10. 48 cubic feet

Post Test 109–110

1.

2. quadrilateral
3. triangular prism
4. A(3, 8); B(9, 8); C(7, 3); D(1, 3)
5. 6
6. 5
7. clockwise turn
8. yes
9. 135 cubic inches
10. 54 square feet

0-7424-2985-7 *Using the Standards: Geometry*

acute angle

edge

equilateral triangle

face

flip

intersecting lines

0-7424-2985-7 *Using the Standards: Geometry*

a line segment
where two faces of
a solid figure meet

an angle that has
a measure less
than 90°

the flat surface of
a solid figure

a triangle with
3 sides of
equal length

lines that cross
each other at
one point

a transformation
that creates a mirror
image of the
original image

0-7424-2985-7 *Using the Standards: Geometry*

isosceles triangle

line

line of symmetry

net

obtuse angle

parallel lines

0-7424-2985-7 *Using the Standards: Geometry*

a path that goes on forever in both directions

a triangle with 2 sides of equal length

a 2-dimensional drawing of the faces of a 3-dimensional solid figure

a line that divides a picture or shape into two halves that are mirror images of each other

lines that do not intersect each other

an angle that has a measure greater than 90°

0-7424-2985-7 *Using the Standards: Geometry*

perpendicular lines

point symmetry

polygon

ray

regular figure

right angle

Published by Instructional Fair. Copyright protected.

0-7424-2985-7 *Using the Standards: Geometry*

when a figure can be turned about a point and look exactly like itself before one complete rotation

lines that intersect to form right angles

part of a line that has one endpoint and goes on forever in the other direction

a closed plane figure with 3 or more sides

an angle that has a measure of 90°

a plane figure that has all sides of equal length and all angles of equal measures

0-7424-2985-7 *Using the Standards: Geometry*

scalene triangle

segment

similar figures

slide

turn

vertex

0-7424-2985-7 *Using the Standards: Geometry*

part of a line
that has
two endpoints

a triangle that
has no sides
of equal
lengths

a transformation that
creates an image
moved from the
location of the original
image

two figures that
have the same shape
and sides that are
proportional to
each other

the point where
two line
segments meet

a transformation
that creates a
rotated image of the
original image

Published by Instructional Fair. Copyright protected.

0-7424-2985-7 *Using the Standards: Geometry*